KID'S P
COOKBOOK

Editor:
Janet M. Stewart

Illustrators:
Rick Rowden
Gord Frazer
Tina Seemann

Copyright © 1988 by Hayes Publishing Ltd.

Printed in Hong Kong

ISBN 0-88625-200-8

CHP BOOKS

3312 Mainway, Burlington, Ontario L7M 1A7, Canada
2045 Niagara Falls Blvd., Unit 14, Niagara Falls, NY 14304, U.S.A.

CONTENTS

ABOUT THIS BOOK

Besides games and prizes, parties are about food - great food, fun food! In this book you'll discover fun ways to make scrumptious food. If you follow the recipes, in a short time you'll be a first class "junior gourmet."

If you're a beginner in the kitchen, get some help from someone with more experience. The recipes with a red light beside them are more difficult than some of the others. Read through the recipe before you begin to make sure you understand it. Then gather up the ingredients and equipment you'll need. Watch carefully for the yellow light. Wherever you see this sign, the method gets a little tricky. If you continue alone, be extra cautious. When you see the green light, read the instructions and then begin. You won't have too much trouble with these recipes.

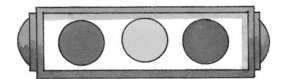

Most measurements in this book are in imperial measure. If you want to convert to metric, use the conversion table at the back of the book. And, if you're unsure about equipment or words used in the recipes, check our well-stocked kitchen on the next page, or the glossary on page 48. You'll find what you need there.

OUR WELL-STOCKED KITCHEN

1. small bowl
2. medium bowl
3. large bowl
4. slotted spoon
5. spatula
6. grapefruit knife
7. knife
8. sifter
9. double boiler
10. wooden spoon
11. ladle
12. skewer
13. toothpick
14. bamboo steamer
15. pastry blender/masher
16. candy thermometer
17. wok
18. scissors
19. oven mitts
20. strainer
21. blender
22. measuring cup
23. pot
24. large pot
25. round pan
26. lemon squeezer
27. electric mixer
28. colander
29. weigh scale
30. skillet/frying pan
31. hand mixer
32. whisk
33. garlic crusher
34. lifter
35. fondue

5

A Real Punchy Party

Parties are time for fun and games! Everyone gets thirsty while playing and will really appreciate a big glass of ice-cold punch. Here are some for you to choose.

Cranky Cranberry Puncher

Ingredients:

- 4 1/2 cups cranberry juice cocktail, chilled
- 1 - 6 ounce can frozen pink lemonade concentrate, thawed
- 9 cups ginger ale, chilled

Method:

In a large punch bowl, mix cranberry juice cocktail and lemonade. Stir in ginger ale. Serve immediately. Makes 25 servings.

Peanut Butter Bonanza

Ingredients:

- 3 cups milk
- 1 cup vanilla ice cream, softened
- 1/2 cup creamy peanut butter
- 3 1/2 oz. package vanilla instant pudding mix

Method:

Combine ingredients in blender. Cover and blend until smooth (about 1 minute). Pour into glasses and serve immediately.

Party Punch

Ingredients:

- 1 can (48 oz.) pineapple juice

- 6 3/4 cups ginger ale
- 1 large container lime sherbert

Method:

Combine all ingredients and add ice. Serve to your guests. This will really quench their thirst!

Fruity Punch

Ingredients:

- 1 can (6 oz.) frozen lemonade concentrate
- 3 - 4 cans water
- 1 can (48 oz.) pineapple juice
- 6 3/4 cups ginger ale or 7-Up (1.5 L)

Method:

In a large punch bowl, mix all ingredients and garnish with orange slices.

Christmas Punch

Ingredients:

- 1 can (12 oz.) frozen orange juice concentrate
- 3 cups cranberry juice cocktail
- 6 cups soda water
- ice cubes

Method:

Pour undiluted orange juice and cranberry juice into a large jug and stir until well blended. Just before serving, pour orange juice mixture into a punch bowl. Add soda water slowly and stir. Top with ice cubes.

Shake it up, Baby!

Basic Milk Shake

Ingredients:

- 2 cups milk
- 1/2 cup ice cream
- 1/2 cup fruit pieces

Method:

Put all ingredients in blender and liquidize.

Serve in tall glasses.

Variations:

If you don't have a blender, use fruit flavoring instead of fruit pieces and mix well. Vary by using different fruits and different flavors of ice cream.

Pink Banana Cocktail

Ingredients:

- 2 cups cranapple drink
- 1 banana
- 2 cups orange juice
- 6 ice cubes

Method:

Mix ingredients in blender and pour into four tall glasses. Serve with straws.

If you want to be fancy, dip the rims of glasses in lemon juice and then into sugar, to add a sweet frosty rim on your glass.

Creamy Yogurt Shakes

Ingredients:

- 3 cups milk
- 1 1/2 cups vanilla ice cream
- 1 cup plain yogurt
- 1/4 cup liquid honey
- 1 1/2 teaspoons vanilla flavoring

Method:

Mix all ingredients in a blender. Pour into tall glasses and serve.

Variation:

Use strawberry ice cream instead of vanilla, and strawberry jam instead of honey.

PARTY PIZZAS

Ingredients:
- English muffins
- 1 can (7 1/2 oz.) pizza tomato sauce
- mozzarella cheese, grated
- oregano

These little pizzas are as much fun to make as they are to eat!

Party Pizza

Ideas for toppings:

Salami, pepperoni, ham, bacon bits, green pepper, sliced mushrooms, sliced onions, pineapple chunks, olives, anchovies.

Method:

Heat oven to 425°F.

Cut muffins in half, spread insides with tomato sauce, and sprinkle with garlic salt, oregano and mozzarella cheese. Top with your choice of two or three toppings and more cheese if desired.

Place on cookie sheet and heat in oven for 7 to 10 minutes or until cheese melts.

Or toast under broiler for a few minutes until bubbly. Serve.

Fruit Pizza

Pizza with a difference! Gather all your favorite fruits - bananas, oranges, grapes, strawberries, raspberries, kiwi, peaches, apples and blueberries. We're going to make a great pizza!

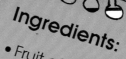

Ingredients:
- Fruit of your choice, whole or sliced
- 8 oz. cream cheese
- 2 tablespoons icing sugar
- 1/2 teaspoon vanilla flavoring
- 1/2 cup marmalade, or peach or apricot jam
- sugar cookie dough (see below)

Method:

Pat cookie dough onto well-greased pizza pan and bake at 375°F for about 10 minutes, until crust is ready.

Cook and loosen with a lifter so that it can be removed easily.

Beat cream cheese to soften, mix in sugar and vanilla, and carefully spread over crust.

Make fun shapes such as animals, stars, happy faces, etc. all over the crust with your fruit.

Heat marmalade or jam until soft and easy to spread. Spoon over fruit to glaze (you may need to add a little water).

Cookie Dough ●

Ingredients:

- 2/3 cup shortening
- 3/4 cup white sugar
- 1 egg
- 1/2 teaspoon vanilla
- 1/2 teaspoon baking powder
- 1/4 teaspoon salt
- 4 teaspoons milk
- 2 cups sifted all-purpose flour

Method:

Preheat oven to 375°F. Cream shortening and sugar, egg and vanilla together in a large bowl until fluffy. Stir in milk. In smaller bowl sift together flour, baking powder, etc.

Stir into creamed mixture. Blend well. Chill for 1 hour. On a lightly floured surface roll out to a quarter of an inch. Cut out shapes. Sprinkle with white sugar. Place on lightly greased cookie sheet. Bake 375°F for 6 - 7 minutes.

Savory Snacks

Roll up your sleeves and get ready. The fun is just beginning.

Bacon Roll-ups

Ingredients:
- 16 slices white bread
- 16 slices bacon
- 1 can cream of mushroom soup
- 32 toothpicks

Method:

Preheat oven to 375°F.

Cut crusts from bread. Flatten the slices slightly with a rolling pin and cut in half lengthwise.

Spread each slice of bread with soup and form into a roll with soup on the inside.

Cut bacon strips in half and wrap around the bread rolls, securing each with a toothpick.

Place bacon rolls on a roasting pan. Bake for 10 minutes, turn over and bake for a further 10 minutes.

Drain any excess grease on paper towel and serve hot.

Variation: Use cheese spread instead of soup.

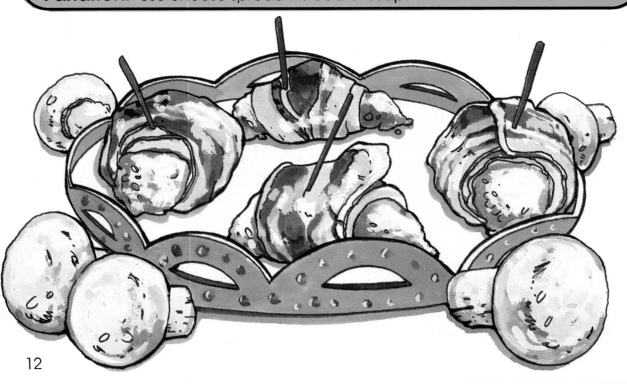

Keep those sleeves up...here comes more messy fun!

Cheese and Sausage Balls

Method:

Heat oven to 375°F.

Using your hands, work all ingredients together until well blended.
Try not to get stuck in the mixture!

Form into small balls, place on a cookie sheet, and flatten slightly with the back of a spoon.

Bake for 10 to 15 minutes or until slightly browned.

Ingredients:

- 3 cups Teabisk or Bisquick
- 1 pound pork sausage meat
- 10 oz. old cheddar cheese, grated

Happy Hawaiian Wieners

This tasty snack is sure to put a smile on everyone's face.

Ingredients:

- 12 wieners
- 1 can pineapple chunks
- toothpicks

Method:

Cut the wieners into bite-sized pieces (about 1/2 inch thick). Take a toothpick and put a piece of wiener and a chunk of pineapple on it.

Make up as many as you like and put them on a cookie sheet.

Bake for 10 minutes at 325° F.

Ingredients:

- boiled ham slices
- cream cheese, softened
- barbecue flavored chips

Hammy Cheese

Method:

Crush chips and add to softened cream cheese.

Spread over ham slices and roll up, jelly-roll style. Secure with toothpick and chill. Cut into pieces, each secured with a toothpick, and serve.

Cheesy Bologna Stacks

Ingredients:

- softened pineapple cream cheese
- bologna slices

Method:

Spread 4 slices of bologna with cheese mixture.

Pile one on top of another, and cover top with fifth slice of bologna.

Wrap in waxed paper and chill for about an hour.

Before serving, cut into small squares, slices, or triangles.

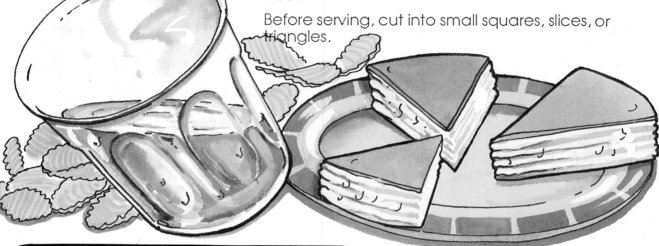

Cheesy Shapes

Method:

Remove crusts from bread. Save the crusts in a brown paper bag. They will harden and can be used for bread crumbs, or you can give them to the birds.

Beat all other ingredients in a large bowl until fluffy. Spread on bread slices and cut into shapes (squares, triangles, diamonds, etc.).

Arrange on a flat cookie sheet. Bake at 350°F for about 10 minutes or until brown.

Serve these yummy cheesy shapes to your party guests. They'll be delighted.

Ingredients:

- 1 loaf white or brown bread, sliced
- 1/2 pound butter, softened
- 1/4 pound cheddar cheese, grated
- 1 egg white
- 1/4 teaspoon salt
- 1/2 teaspoon paprika
- 1 tablespoon table cream
- 1 teaspoon garlic powder
- small, cooked bacon pieces (optional)

Tastie Toastie Bites

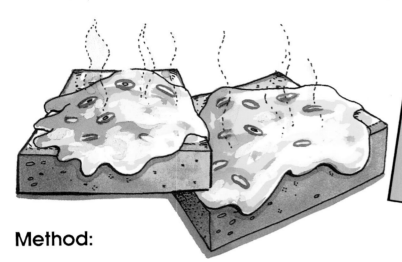

Ingredients:

- 1 1/2 cups mayonnaise
- 1/4 cup mozzarella cheese
- 1 medium onion, diced
- Parmesan cheese
- 1 loaf rye bread, white or brown

Method:

Toast one side of the slices of bread under the broiler.

Mix mayonnaise, cheese and onion together until blended.

Spread on untoasted side of bread.

Sprinkle with Parmesan cheese and cut into squares or fingers. Lay on flat cookie sheet. Broil under broiler until bubbly and browned. Keep a close watch - they cook quickly!

These are tasty on pumpernickel bread, but only toast one side.

Bouncy Bagels

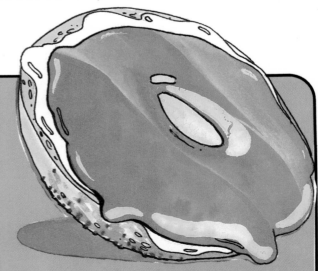

Slice bagels in half, then cut in half again to make crescent shapes.
Spread lightly with butter and top with grated cheddar cheese.
Grill in toaster oven or under broiler until cheese melts.

Variations:

Toast sliced bagels, then spread with cream cheese. (Top with your favorite jam, if desired.)
Toast sliced bagels, then top with tuna, ham or egg salad.

16

Cheese and Pineapple Spikes

Ingredients:

- 1 small can pineapple chunks
- cheddar cheese (enough for about 20 cubes)
- cherries (maraschino or glazed)
- cocktail sticks
- 1 large potato OR 1/2 orange or grapefruit

Method:

Wrap potato in foil and put in middle of large serving plate.

OR

Place 1/2 large orange or grapefruit as a centerpiece on a large serving plate. Carefully open can of pineapple and drain the juice off thoroughly.
Cut the cheese into fat cubes.

Skewer pieces of cheese and pineapple onto cocktail sticks. Top with cherry and stick into the potato or orange.

This spiky treat will be a success at any party!

Variations:

Use cubes of ham, stuffed olives, cocktail onions, or mandarin orange sections.

Play around and add a variety of mouth-watering goodies all on one cocktail stick.

Tangy Balls of Meat

Meatball ingredients:
- 1 pound ground beef
- 1 egg, slightly beaten
- 1 onion, finely minced
- 1 teaspoon salt
- dash pepper

Sauce ingredients:
- 1 bottle (12 oz.) chili sauce
- 1 jar (10 oz.) grape jelly
- 2 tablespoons lemon juice
- dash Worcestershire sauce

Method:

Mix ingredients for meatballs in a large bowl. Roll into small, bite-size meatballs and set aside.

In a large skillet combine sauce ingredients and heat until bubbling.

Add meatballs to the sauce. Cook slowly for 1 hour. Stir occasionally to glaze the meatballs.

Serve on toothpicks for a treat your friends will love! But have paper towels handy; these are a bit messy to eat!

Easy Chicken Wings - Microwave

Ingredients:

- 2 pounds chicken wings
- 1 package Italian style chicken coating mix

Method:

Wash and dry chicken wings. Very carefully cut off tips of wings and discard.

Cut wings in half at joint and coat with chicken mix, according to package directions.

Place the chicken in a round 9" plate or casserole.

Cover loosely with waxed paper.

Microwave on HIGH 1-2 minutes for each chicken wing. Turn chicken pieces halfway through cooking time. Stand time - 5 minutes, uncovered.

Potato Skins

Method:

Scrub and prick potatoes. Rub with oil. Bake for 1 hour at 400°F or until cooked (when a fork is poked into the potato and it comes out clean). Let the potatoes cool. Cut potatoes in half lengthwise. Then slice in half again. Scoop out inside of potato, leaving a shell about 1/4" thick (make sure they aren't too thin). Melt butter or margarine and brush onto both sides of the potato skins. Arrange skins on an ungreased cookie sheet and bake at 500°F for 12 minutes, or until crisp.

Remove carefully from oven with oven mitts and sprinkle with cheese and bacon bits. Return to oven for 2 - 3 minutes, or until cheese melts. Serve with sour cream.

Ingredients:

- 4 medium/large potatoes
- 4 tablespoons melted butter or margarine
- 1/2 cup grated chedder cheese
- 1/2 cup sour cream
- bacon bits

19

WILD VEGGIE PLATTER

Pick out a bunch of different vegetables like carrots, celery, cauliflower, broccoli, beans, zucchini...or whatever you like. After you've washed them, break them into different shapes and sizes. If your parents or older brothers and sisters are around, have them help you cut the veggies into shapes like cauliflowerettes, broccoli florets, zucchini slices, cut green beans or carrot sticks.

If you're old enough to use a knife, carefully cut out some wild designs of your own.

Cold Veggie Platter

Arrange your veggie shapes on a large plate and put it out for all your friends to enjoy. They can munch and crunch while playing games!

Hot Veggie Platter

Microwave Method:

Arrange your veggie shapes on a large, round microwave-safe plate.

Cover with plastic wrap and microwave at HIGH for 6 minutes. Remove from microwave and unwrap. Careful -- it's hot! Dot with pieces of butter and sprinkle with 2 tablespoons of Parmesan cheese. Cover again with plastic wrap and let stand for 5 minutes before serving.

Not quite as crunchy, but great munching!

DIP-A-DEE-DO-DA!

Dips go great with fruit, vegetables, crackers, bread, or...use your imagination and dip into it with whatever catches your fancy!

Orange and Peanut Dip

Ingredients:

- 1/2 cup peanut butter
- 1/4 cup orange juice
- 1/2 cup sour cream

Method:

Mix ingredients together in a small bowl. Serve with your choice of fruits: pear and apple wedges, strawberries, canteloupe or melon.

Yummy Yogurt Dip

Ingredients:

- 1 cup plain yogurt
- 2 tablespoons brown sugar
- 1 tablespoon orange juice
- 1/2 teaspoon grated orange rind

Method:

Blend ingredients together and refrigerate for 30 minutes before serving. Serve with fresh fruit - apples, bananas, orange sections, apricot halves or pineapple chunks.

This light, fluffy, cheesy dip makes eating vegetables great fun!

Cheese in a Cloud

Ingredients:

- 1/2 cup mayonnaise
- 1/2 cup sour cream
- 1/4 cup Parmesan cheese
- pepper, garlic and chives to taste

(Double or triple your recipe if you're having a lot of guests.)

Method:

With a wooden spoon, mix the mayonnaise and sour cream together in a medium-size bowl. Add cheese, garlic, pepper and chives. Mix the ingredients together until blended. If you want to spice it up even more, add a pinch of cayenne pepper.

Your braver guests will love it!

UMMM... MEXICAN!

You might want your party to have a particular theme. One great idea that's always been popular is the Mexican theme. Tacos, taco salad, rice - even Mexican hot chocolate. Everyone will remember your party for a long time to come.

Tacos (simple method)

Ingredients:

- 1 pound ground beef
- 1 package taco seasoning
- 1 package taco shells

Method:

In a large skillet, brown ground beef and break into small pieces. Drain off fat. Add seasonings and water. Simmer 15 - 20 minutes. Fill taco shells with meat mixture and add your choice of toppings.

Toppings (have prepared in separate dishes):

Chopped lettuce, tomatoes, olives, green onions, shredded cheddar cheese, sour cream and mayonnaise.

If you think you're a really good chef, try making your taco meat stuffing and hot sauce from scratch! This will impress your parents as well as your friends.

Tacos (from scratch)

Method:

In a large skillet, brown beef over MEDIUM-HIGH heat until crumbly. Drain off fat. Add remaining ingredients and mix well. Cook over MEDIUM-LOW heat until water is evaporated (approximately 25-30 minutes).

Meanwhile, prepare your hot sauce.

Beef mixture ingredients:

- 1 pound ground beef
- 1 teaspoon salt
- 2 teaspoons cumin seed
- 1/2 teaspoon garlic powder
- 1/2 teaspoon onion powder
- 1/4 cup cornmeal
- 1 tablesppon chili powder
- 1 cup water

Hot sauce ingredients:

- 2 oz. pimentos
- 1 teaspoon crushed chilies
- 1 teaspoon onion powder
- 1/2 teaspoon garlic powder
- 1 teaspoon salt
- 1/3 cup water
- 2 1-inch cubes cheddar cheese
- 1 - 5 1/2 oz. tin tomato paste

Method:

Combine all sauce ingredients in a blender at HIGH speed. Transfer sauce into small saucepan and heat through for several minutes.

Taco ingredients:

- 1 package taco shells
- 1/2 cup cheddar cheese, grated
- 1 cup shredded lettuce
- beef mixture
- hot sauce

Method:

Fill taco shells with beef mixture. Spoon hot sauce over the meat and top with the grated cheese and shredded lettuce. Serve with rice and tossed salad.

Crunchy Fresh Taco Salad

Method:

In a large skillet, brown ground beef and break up into small pieces. Carefully drain off fat and let cool. Wash and dry lettuce and break it into bite-size pieces in a large glass bowl. Add the next five ingredients and the ground beef. Mix well. Combine mayonnaise with taco sauce. Just before serving, add the mayonnaise mixture and crushed chips to the bowl of lettuce. Toss well and serve.

Ingredients:
- 1 pound ground beef
- 1 head iceberg lettuce
- 1 can red kidney beans, drained
- 1 small onion, diced
- 1 tomato, diced
- 1 avocado, diced
- 1 cup cheddar cheese, grated
- 1 1/2 cups mayonnaise
- 3 tablespoons mild taco sauce
- 1 package nacho chips, crushed

Mexican Rice Delight

Ingredients:

- 1 cup rice
- 2 tablespoons shortening
- 1/2 onion, chopped finely
- 1/2 teaspoon garlic salt
- 1 small can tomato paste
- 1/2 teaspoon salt
- 1/2 teaspoon sugar
- 1/4 teaspoon pepper

Method:

In a large skillet, melt shortening and saute/simmer rice until golden. You might need your parents or older brother or sister to help you with this. If you try it alone be extra careful. Add onion and garlic and saute until golden. Stir in tomato paste and 1 cup of hot water, salt, sugar and pepper; bring to a boil. Reduce heat. Cook without stirring until rice is tender and fluffy. Add more water if needed to keep rice from sticking to bottom of pan. Transfer into a serving dish. Serve with taco chips or salad.

Mexican Hot Chocolate

Method:

In a large saucepan, heat chocolate chips, water, cinnamon and salt over LOW heat, stirring constantly until chocolate is melted and mixture is smooth. Heat to boiling on MEDIUM-HIGH heat. Reduce heat and stir in milk. Heat through for a few minutes, but be careful you don't burn the mixture. Add almond flavoring and beat with a hand beater or whisk until foamy. Serve immediately in large mugs. Your friends will certainly be impressed!

Ingredients:

- 4 oz. semi-sweet chocolate chips
- 1 cup water
- 1 teaspoon ground cinnamon
- 1/4 teaspoon salt
- 5 cups milk
- 1/2 teaspoon almond extract

GET POPPIN!

With or without a popcorn popper, popping corn is easy! If you're using a machine, follow the manufacturer's instructions. Some of the machines use oil, some will pop on air!

● Stovetop Popcorn

Ingredients:

- 2 tablespoons oil
- 1/2 cup popping corn
- 1/4 cup melted butter
- salt to taste

Method:

If you're using a pot on top of the stove, be careful! You only need enough oil to cover the bottom of the pot. Turn the burner to HIGH and drop a couple of corn kernels into the pot. Put the lid on. When you hear them pop, carefully add the rest of the kernels and put the lid back on. Jiggle the pot over the burner a bit so the kernels are in the oil as flat as possible. After 1 minute, turn the heat down to MEDIUM. Jiggle the pot again. After another minute, turn the heat off and jiggle the pot again quickly. Carefully remove the pot from the stove with an oven mitt and dump the popcorn into a big bowl. Add butter and salt and you're ready to go!

Peanut Butter Delight

Give your guests a treat with this yummy popcorn!

Ingredients:

- 4 tablespoons peanut butter
- 6 tablespoons butter or magarine

Method:

Melt ingredients together in a small pan over LOW heat, pour over popcorn and mix well.

Bacon Popcorn

Ingredients:

- 1 cup bacon bits
- 1 cup butter or margarine

Method:

Melt butter or margarine in a small pan over LOW heat. Stir in bacon bits, pour over popcorn and mix well.

Caramel Corn

Ingredients:

- 1 cup corn syrup, or 1 cup caramel candy
- 1/2 cup butter or margarine

Method:

Melt butter or margarine over LOW heat in small saucepan. Add corn syrup or caramels and stir until melted. Pour over popcorn. Mix well.

Or...add your own ideas, such as cheese, taco flavor, etc. and serve original scrumptious popcorn to surprise your friends.

FANTASTIC FONDUES!

Fondues are as fun as any game for large or small parties. But be careful when you're dipping. Don't drip on your party clothes!

Chocolate Fondue

Ingredients:

- 7 oz. chocolate chips or 6 squares semi-sweet chocolate
- 1 1/2 cups sugar
- 1 cup evaporated milk
- 1/2 cup butter
- dash salt
- 1 tablespoon orange juice (optional)

Method:

Put 1 cup cold water in bottom pan of double boiler. Place the chocolate chips or squares in the top pan. Bring water just to boiling on HIGH heat; then reduce heat to very low and add top pan, stirring chocolate until melted. Add butter, sugar, salt and slowly pour in the milk. Stir until all are blended and smooth. Heat may have to be slightly increased here to speed things up. Transfer chocolate mixture to a chocolate fondue pot, and get ready to dip in your choice of fruit, cut-up cake (angel or sponge), marshmallows, or whatever else you or your guests might like.

Suggestions for fruits:

- 2 bananas, sliced
- 2 apples, sliced
- 2 pears, sliced
- mandarin orange sections
- grapes, melon balls, strawberries, cantaloupe

NOTE: Do not use your regular fondue pot for these "sweet fondue" recipes. Use only an onion soup bowl or fireproof dish over a candle or special chocolate fondue pot.

Strawberry or Raspberry Fondue

Ingredients:

- 2 10 oz. packages frozen strawberries or raspberries, thawed
- 1/4 cup cornstarch
- 2 tablespoons sugar
- 1/2 cup water
- 1 4 oz. container whipped cream cheese, softened

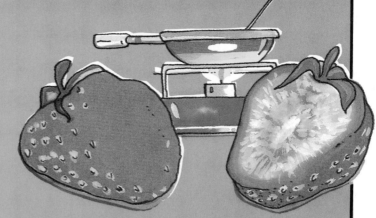

Method:

In a saucepan, mash berrries slightly. In a teacup, blend together cornstarch, sugar and water. Mix until smooth. Add to berries. Cook over MEDIUM heat and stir until thickened and bubbly. Add cream cheese, stirring until melted. Pour into fondue pot to serve.

Creamy Vanilla Fondue

Ingredients:

- 1/2 cup butter
- 1 cup sugar
- 1/2 cup light cream
- 1 teaspoon vanilla

Method:

In a small saucepan, melt butter over MEDIUM heat. Add remaining ingredients and mix well. Heat to simmer, stirring constantly, about 5 minutes - or until sugar has dissolved. Pour into fondue pot.

SWEETS AND TASTY TREATS

While finger foods, tacos and shakes are just fine, no party can survive without something sweet, something special. Pick from the recipes outlined over the next few pages to make a treat all your friends will like. You can use these recipes to surprise your parents or grandparents on a special day by giving them a special treat, too!

Fruity Yogurt Jellies

Ingredients:

- 1 package raspberry jelly powder
- 1/2 cup hot water
- 1/2 cup cold water
- 3 5 oz. cartons raspberry yogurt

Method:

Put jelly in small bowl, add half cup hot water, and stir until dissolved. Add half cup cold water and stir. Cool but do not set. Add yogurt to jelly mixture and stir with wooden spoon until well blended. Pour into small dishes and refrigerate until set. Also try strawberry and orange flavors. Serve with a variety of cookies and squares.

Very easy to make, but what a delicious treat!

32

Colorful miniature marshmallows and bits of fruit make this salad a favorite for everyone!

Marshmallow Salad

Method:

Mix all ingredients well in a glass bowl. Cover with plastic wrap and refrigerate for 24 hours before serving at your party!

Ingredients:

- 1 small can mandarin oranges, drained
- 1 cup pineapple tidbits (or fruit cocktail) drained
- 1 cup coconut, flaked
- 1 cup colored miniature marshmallows
- 2 cups sour cream

Nanaimo Bars

Method:

In a double boiler, heat butter, sugar and cocoa until melted. Stir in beaten egg and remove from heat. Add crumbs, coconut and nuts and mix well. Spread in 8" square greased pan and refrigerate.

Base:

- 1/2 cup butter
- 1/4 cup white sugar
- 3 tablespoons cocoa
- 1 1/2 cups Graham cracker crumbs
- 1 egg, slightly beaten
- 1 cup coconut
- 1/2 cup chopped walnuts
- 1 teaspoon vanilla

Filling:

- 2 cups icing sugar
- 1/4 cup butter
- 2 tablespoons custard powder
- 2 tablespoons hot water

Method:

Combine all ingredients in a small bowl and mix well with electric mixer. Spread evenly over the chilled chocolate base and return to refrigerator.

Topping:

- 2 squares semi-sweet chocolate
- 1 teaspoon butter

Method:

Melt together in double boiler or microwave and stir until smooth. Spread evenly over chilled filling and chill again. Cut into small squares for serving.

Crispy Crunchie Bars

Ingredients:

- 1 cup white sugar
- 1 cup corn syrup
- 1 cup smooth peanut butter
- 6 cups rice crispies

Method:

Cook sugar and corn syrup in a large saucepan, stirring all the time, until mixture begins to bubble.

Remove from heat and stir in peanut butter and rice crispies. Stir thoroughly and quickly, as the mixture sets and gets sticky very quickly. Pour into greased 9x13-inch pan and press down evenly with back of wooden spoon or with your hands, moistened with warm water. Top with colored sprinkles. Cool. Cut into squares to serve.

Crispy Rice Squares

Ingredients:

- 5 cups rice crispies
- 4 cups marshmallows
- 1/4 cup melted butter or margarine
- 1/2 teaspoon vanilla

Method:

Melt the butter/margarine in a fair-sized pot over LOW heat. Add the marshmallows, stirring continuously with a wooden spoon. When the marshmallows are melted, turn the burner off and remove your pot from the stove using oven mitts. Immediately add rice crispies and coat them with the marshmallow mixture. Spread out mixture in flat 9x13-inch pan - flatten - chill.

Variation:

Use miniature fruit-flavored marshmallows for a real fruity-flavored crispy square!

Ingredients:

- 1 cup chocolate chips
- 1/4 cup margarine
- 1/4 cup icing sugar
- 1 egg
- 1 1/2 cup Graham cracker crumbs
- 1/2 cup chopped nuts (optional)
- peppermint flavoring (a few drops)

Mint Chocolate Squares

Method:

Melt chocolate chips and margarine in a double boiler, stirring until melted. Mix in icing sugar, egg and peppermint and beat well with wooden spoon. Stir in crumbs and nuts. Pour into greased 8" square pan. Press down evenly and chill.

Ingredients:

- 1/4 cup margarine or butter
- 2 cups icing sugar
- 2 tablespoons milk
- green food coloring

Topping for Mint Chocolate Squares

Method:

Cream butter with electric mixer in a small bowl. Slowly add icing sugar, mixing at low speed. Add enough milk to make it smooth and easy to spread. Mix in a few drops of coloring to make a light green topping. Spread topping evenly over chilled base. Decorate with chocolate chips or sprinkles, if desired, and cut into squares to serve.

Candy apples are fun to make and could be used as prizes at your party. Follow the recipes and, when the apples are done, wrap them in waxed paper and tie ribbons around them. They'll look good enough to eat!

Ingredients:
- 6 apples
- 6 wooden skewers or popsicle sticks
- 1 1/3 cups sugar
- 2 cups light corn syrup
- 1/4 teaspoon red food coloring

Candy Apples

Method:

Wash apples and remove stems. Push skewers or popsicle sticks into apples. Set off to one side.

Combine sugar, corn syrup, food coloring in top of double boiler. Cook over LOW heat, stirring constantly until the sugar has dissolved (about 4 minutes). Cover and simmer for another 8 minutes.

Then uncover and cook without stirring until mixture is at 300°F (hard crack stage). Use a candy thermometer if you have one. Turn off heat. Quickly take each apple and dunk in syrup until dripping. Let the excess drip off into the pot.

Then put the apples on buttered cookie sheet to cool (or use waxed paper). Once chilled, you can wrap them in waxed paper and tie them with a ribbon.

Your guests will be delighted!

Honey Yogurt Squares

Filling Ingredients:

- 1 envelope gelatin
- 1 cup fruit-flavored yogurt
- 1 8 oz. package cream cheese
- 3 tablespoons honey
- 1/2 teaspoon vanilla flavoring
- 1/4 teaspoon lemon juice
- 1/4 cup hot water

Crust Ingredients:

- 2 cups Graham crackers crumbs
- 1/2 cup melted butter
- 2 tablespoons honey

Method:

Make crust by melting butter and honey and adding to crumbs in a large bowl. Mix well and press into buttered 8" square pan. Chill.

To make filling:

Beat cream cheese and yogurt together in medium- size bowl with electric mixer until smooth. Add honey, vanilla and juice and continue beating until creamy. Dissolve gelatin in hot water and stir into creamy mixture until just mixed. Pour filling over crumb crust and chill before serving. Cut into squares to serve. Dip knife in hot water while cutting squares to prevent sticking.

Peanut Butter Treats

Ingredients:

- 4 squares semi-sweet chocolate
- 1/2 cup smooth peanut butter
- peanuts (optional)
- paper baking cups

Method:

Melt chocolate in a double boiler. Add peanut butter and stir until melted.

Spoon into small paper baking cups until three-quarters full, and top with a peanut if desired.

Chill before serving.

Bars of Mars

Method:

Melt Mars bars and margarine together in a large saucepan over MEDIUM heat, stirring occasionally.

Remove from heat and stir in rice crispies. Spoon into a greased 8" square pan and pack down firmly. Chill. Melt chocolate in double boiler, add butter and stir.

Spread over chilled base in pan and chill again.

Cut into squares and serve.

Ingredients:

- 3 Mars bars, regular size
- 3 oz. margarine or butter
- 3 cups rice crispies
- 2 squares semi-sweet chocolate
- 1 teaspoon butter

A candy delight for any party!

Ingredients:

- 1 1/2 cups icing sugar
- 1/2 cup butter
- 1/2 cup cocoa
- 1/2 cup chocolate chips

● Easy Truffles

Method:

Cream butter in a small bowl and slowly add the icing sugar and cocoa. Shape the mixture into small balls and roll them in chocolate chips.

Chill and they're ready for your party.

Truffles with a difference

Ingredients:

- 2 tablespoons coconut
- 2 tablespoons cocoa
- 2 oz. butter
- 8 crushed digestive cookies/biscuits
- 1/2 can condensed milk

Method:

Melt butter with milk in a small saucepan over MEDIUM heat. Add cocoa, coconut and biscuit crumbs. Turn heat off and pour mixture into a small bowl. Refrigerate until cool.

Then the fun begins! Roll into balls and coat in chocolate chips.

Serve to your guests - they'll disappear in minutes.

Marshmallows in a Cup of Chocolate!

Method:

Melt 3 or 4 chocolate squares over LOW heat in the top of a double boiler. Remove from heat. Fill bottom of paper baking cups with two teaspoons of chocolate.

Quickly place a large marshmallow into the chocolate in the paper baking cup and leave to harden.

Decorate the top of the marshmallow with a dab of chocolate and cherries, nuts, silver balls, candy or whatever else you like. These pretty treats look great on the table as favors. You could also make them into place names by tying a small ribbon with a name card around the marshmallow.

MORE THAN A TRIFLE DESSERT...

Easy to make and yummy to eat, trifles are a hit at any party!

Scottish Trifle

Ingredients:

- 1 large jam roll, sliced
- 1 large package vanilla instant pudding
- 1 cup whipped cream or 1 package whipped topping mix
- chocolate flakes, glace cherries or other decorative toppings of your choice
- 1 3 1/2 oz. package raspberry jelly powder
- 1 19 oz. can fruit cocktail (or peaches or pears)

Method:

Arrange the slices of jam roll over the bottom and up the sides of a glass bowl. Prepare the jelly powder according to package instructions, but use the juice from the canned fruit with the cup of cold water. Pour the liquid jelly over the jam roll slices and refrigerate until set.

Arrange fruit over chilled jelly. Make instant pudding according to package directions and pour over fruit. Chill until ready to serve.

Just before serving, whip the cream or prepare topping and use to completely cover the pudding layer. Decorate with chocolate vermicelli, chocolate flakes, colored niblets or glace cherries.

Creamy Delicious Chocolate Fudge

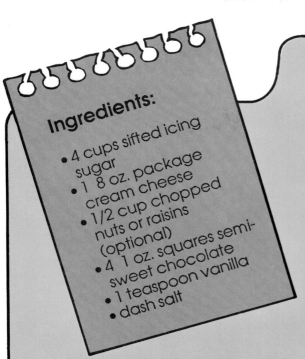

Ingredients:

- 4 cups sifted icing sugar
- 1 8 oz. package cream cheese
- 1/2 cup chopped nuts or raisins (optional)
- 4 1 oz. squares semi-sweet chocolate
- 1 teaspoon vanilla
- dash salt

Method:

Slowly and carefully add sugar to softened cream cheese in a large bowl. Mix well until blended.

Melt chocolate in a double boiler over LOW heat.

Add nuts or raisins to the chocolate and blend in with the cream cheese mixture. Stir in the remaining ingredients.

Press into a greased 8-inch square pan.

Chill overnight. Cut into squares and serve. Refrigerate any leftovers.

PANDA PARTY CAKE

Use any packaged cake mix to make one round cake and one square or rectangular cake. Follow the instructions on the package. If you prefer to make your cake from scratch, follow the recipe below.

Gramma's White Cake

Ingredients:

- 2 cups all-purpose flour
- 2 eggs
- 1/4 cup sugar
- 1 cup milk
- 2 teaspoons baking powder
- 1 teaspoon vanilla
- pinch of salt
- 1/2 cup butter or margarine

Method:

Cream the butter or margarine with the two eggs and beat well with whisk or electric mixer. Add milk and beat again. Slowly sift in flour, sugar and baking powder. Mix together. Add vanilla and a pinch of salt. Blend together. Pour into one round and one square greased cake pan and bake in preheated oven at 375° F for 10 minutes. Then turn oven down to 325° F and bake for 10 - 15 minutes more.

Tip: To see if cake is done, gently pull out oven rack with oven mitt and insert a toothpick into cake's center. If it's clean when pulled out, cake is done. If not, leave the cake to bake for another minute or two.

Frosting

Ingredients:

- 1/4 cup soft butter or margarine
- 2 cups icing sugar
- 1/2 teaspoon vanilla
- 1/4 cup milk

Method:

Soften butter in a medium-size bowl. Add 1/3 of the sugar to butter and cream together. Add vanilla and milk alternately with sugar. Beat with an electric mixer until smooth. Refrigerate until ready to use.

If you aren't very good at making icing, you might want to buy a can of ready-made frosting from your local grocery store. This would also save time if you're in a rush!

44

Putting Your Panda Cake together...

As soon as your cakes have cooled, you can begin your creation! Use a long tray, cookie sheet or thick cardboard covered with tinfoil as your base. Place the round cake on it. Cut a similar round piece from the square cake and place it on the tray, too. This will be your panda's head. Use the extra pieces for the two ears and four paws.

Make them any shape you like. Before you put them on the panda, ice the two round cakes with your white frosting. Save about half a cup of icing for your panda's ears and paws.

Once you've iced your panda, arrange the paws and ears as shown in the picture. Before you ice them, add a tablespoon of cocoa to the icing that's left. Mix it well and you'll have chocolate paws and ears. When you've finished with the paws and ears, use things like cherries or candies (smarties) to make eyes, a nose and mouth.

Licorice can be used to make the claws. When you've finished, your panda will be ready to go and will look so good you won't want to eat it.

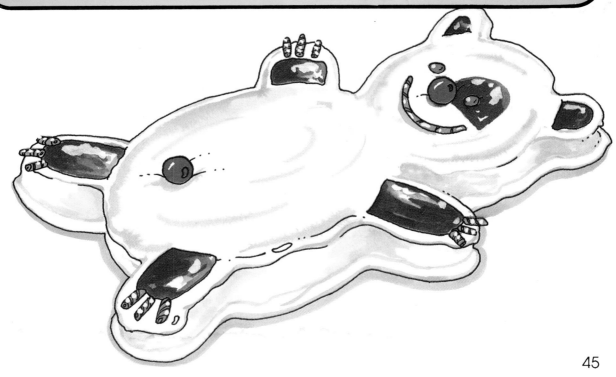

PAMELA'S PARTY PICNIC

When the weather's nice, it's great fun to have a party picnic! Your friends will love the idea - whether it's the park or just your backyard. Any picnic can be successful with the right food. Make up the recipes outlined here and you'll be sure to have a great party picnic!

Baked Chicken Delight

Ingredients:

- 15 chicken pieces, approximately (wings, drumsticks, breasts)
- 1 package Shake & Bake Chicken Coating Mix

Method:

Wash chicken and let most of the water drain off. Then follow the instructions on the Shake & Bake package and bake the chicken for the time required. Once the chicken is done and cooled, wrap it in tinfoil and set it aside for your picnic.

Ingredients:

- 1 cabbage
- 6 - 10 medium-size carrots
- 1/2 cup red/purple cabbage
- 1 lemon
- 2 cups mayonnaise
- 1 cup white vinegar
- 1 clove garlic, crushed
- 1 teaspoon pepper
- 1 teaspoon cayenne pepper

Crunchy Fresh Coleslaw

Method:

Wash cabbage and carrots. Dry them off as best you can. Cut cabbage into 4 or 6 pieces and remove the core. You might need some help with this. Peel or brush the carrots and cut the ends off carefully.

Use a grater to grate the carrots and cabbage into a large bowl. Then shred the red/purple cabbage into the same bowl.

In a separate bowl combine the mayonnaise, vinegar, pepper, garlic and cayenne pepper. Cut the lemon and squeeze the juice into this mixture. Mix it and add to the cabbage mixture. Combine with a wooden spoon.

Potato Salad

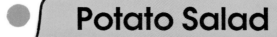

Ingredients:

- potatoes
- eggs
- mayonnaise
- garlic, crushed clove OR 1 teaspoon garlic powder
- onions (optional)
- paprika

Method:

Boil in a large pot of water at least one potato per person and one egg for every two people at your party. The potatoes should be covered with water. Since the eggs don't take as long as the potatoes to cook, add the eggs to the boiling water about 20 minutes after the potatoes. If you cut the potatoes into halves or quarters, they will cook faster. After 35 - 40 minutes, check to see if the potatoes are done by inserting a fork in them. If the fork slides out easily the potatoes are done.

Carefully take the pot to the sink using an oven mitt and pour the water out. Remove the shells from the eggs and, if you don't like the skin of the potatoe, remove it with a small knife. Cut the potatoes into bite-size pieces and cut up the eggs. Put both into a large bowl, and when they've cooled, add mayonnaise a tablespoon at a time, the garlic and onions. When the potatoes are creamy enough for you, sprinkle a bit of paprika over the top of them - it makes them look tasty. Keep the potato salad in an airtight container for your picnic.

Pink Lemonade

Use a couple of cans of pink lemonade from your local grocery store and mix according to package directions. Or if you prefer, make your own lemonade from the following recipe.

Ingredients:

- 1 1/2 cups sugar
- 9 cups water
- 2 cups lemon juice
- 1 cup chilled pineapple or orange juice

Method:

Combine all the ingredients in a plastic pitcher or jug and stir until sugar dissolves. Refrigerate until you leave for your picnic. Keep the lemonade in a thermos jug, if you have one, to keep it cold while you and your guests play through the party!

Dessert...

Bring along some fresh strawberries and sponge cake. If you have a cooler, bring a can of whipped cream. Ummm...good!

Don't forget nice, fresh crusty buns...and watermelon, of course!

Metric Conversions

Measurements in this book are given in imperial measure. Temperatures are in degrees Fahrenheit. Baking pan measurements are given in inches. If you require the metric measurements, this conversion table can be used to make the conversions.

Teaspoons (tsp.) / Tablespoons (tbsp.)

1/4 tsp.	1 mL
1/2 tsp.	2 mL
1 tsp.	5 mL
2 tsps.	10 mL
1 tbsp.	15 mL

Cups

1/4 cup	50 mL
1/3 cup	75 mL
1/2 cup	125 mL
2/3 cup	150 mL
3/4 cup	175 mL
1 cup	250 mL

Ounces - Weight

1 oz.	30 grams
2 oz.	55 grams
3 oz.	85 grams
4 oz.	125 grams
5 oz.	140 grams
6 oz.	170 grams
7 oz.	200 grams
8 oz.	250 grams
16 oz.	500 grams
32 oz.	1000 grams

Oven Temperatures degrees

Fahrenheit	Celcius
275	135
300	150
325	163
350	177
375	190
400	205
425	218
450	233

Pans

8 x 8 inches	20 x 20 cm
9 x 9 inches	22 x 22 cm
9 x 13 inches	22 x 33 cm

GLOSSARY

Alternately
Add portions of different ingredients, one after the other.

Beat
Mix well with an electric mixer, whisk or wooden spoon.

Boil
Cook food in liquid on HIGH heat with bubbles rising continuously, breaking at the surface.

Broil
Cook by exposing food to direct heat under the broiler in the oven.

Brown
Cook in pot until brown on stove top at MEDIUM-HIGH heat or in a very hot oven.

Cream
Mix together or beat with a wooden spoon or electric mixer until light and fluffy or soft and smooth.

Dash/Pinch
Add less than 1/4 teaspoon.

Dry ingredients
Solid ingredients like flour, sugar, baking powder, etc.

Egg white
Inside part of egg separate from yolk.

Fold in
With a gentle up-and-over movement, combine ingredient(s) into a creamed mixture using a wooden spoon or rubber spatula.

Garnish
Decorate finished food on plate with parsley or other piece of food.

Grate
Grind into small pieces by rubbing or scraping on a food grater.

Grease
Grease a baking tray or cookie sheet with butter, margarine, or shortening so the food won't stick to the bottom while baking.

Liquid ingredients
Fluid ingredients like eggs, vanilla flavoring, milk, water, juice, etc.

Liquidize
To beat, blend or boil to change an ingredient from a solid or semi-solid to a liquid.

Melt
Heat ingredients together over a very LOW heat to change from a solid to a liquid.

Peel
Remove the outer skin or layer of a piece of food with a knife or special peeler.

Saute
Cook in frying pan in a small amount of butter, fat or oil.

Sift
Put any ingredients through a sieve or sifter.

Sieve
A round frame, with wire mesh and a handle, to strain foods.

Simmer
Cook food in a liquid just below boiling on a very LOW heat. Bubbles form slowly and break below the surface.

Toss
Mix or toss by turning the ingredients over and over with two forks or two spoons.

Whip
Beat vigorously until fluffy or stiff.

Whisk
Combine ingredients together with a wire whisk, using a circular or side-to-side motion.